Presented to

_____

by

_____

on

_____

11 10 09 08 07 06   9 8 7 6 5 4 3 2 1

stories retold by Susan L. Lingo

illustrated by Kathy Parks

Standard®
PUBLISHING
Bringing The Word to Life

Cincinnati, Ohio

Contents

Story Time Rhyme

(to the tune of "The Mulberry Bush")

Let's join the kids

in the neighborhood

and learn why God

is great and good.

We'll meet new friends and

share our love,

and learn of God above!

Hi! It's me, Night-Light,
your firefly friend!

I can't wait to learn about
God with my friends.
What fun! And if you
look closely, you'll see
me in one of the
pictures of every
story you read.
Let's start reading
together now!

Name Game

God said, "I have called you by name." Isaiah 43:1

Mia Chang had a new kitten. It had long black fur. It had big yellow eyes. And it had the fluffiest tail Mia had ever seen! But the kitten didn't have a name.

"Why don't you call him 'Fluffy'?" said Sophie Springly. But Max Popple didn't like that. "Aww, that's a sissy name!" said Max. "How about calling him 'Max'?"

Mia laughed. "One Max is enough around here! I want a name that's just right." Just then, Jimmy Lopez rode up on his pony, Schnickelfritz. "Now there's a funny name!" laughed Max.

But Jimmy said, "Hey! 'Schnickelfritz' is a way to say 'little friend' in German. My grandpa told me that!"

Sophie sighed. "It's hard thinking up names. Do you think anyone knows all the names in the world?"

"God does," said Max. "God knows everyone's name because God made us. God even knows the name of your kitten before you do, Mia!"

What animals do you see?

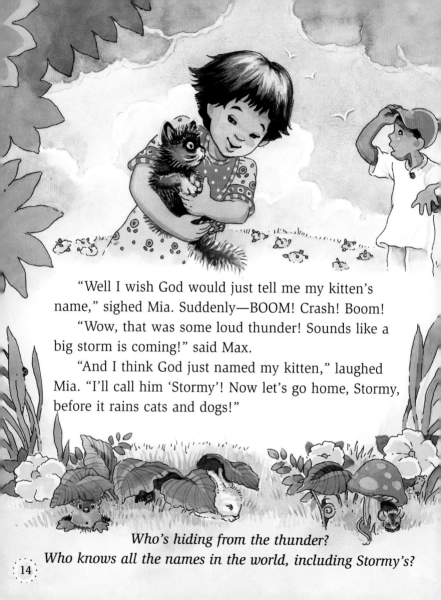

"Well I wish God would just tell me my kitten's name," sighed Mia. Suddenly—BOOM! Crash! Boom!

"Wow, that was some loud thunder! Sounds like a big storm is coming!" said Max.

"And I think God just named my kitten," laughed Mia. "I'll call him 'Stormy'! Now let's go home, Stormy, before it rains cats and dogs!"

Who's hiding from the thunder?
Who knows all the names in the world, including Stormy's?

A Bible Story to Remember

Genesis 2:18-23; 3:20

God told Adam to give all the animals special names. We have special names, too. And God knows all of our names because he made us and he loves us. What's your name? Did you know God has an extra-special name for you? He calls you "his" because you belong to him!

A Prayer to Pray

Dear God,
I'm glad you call us
each by name.
You know and
love us all the same.
Amen.

A Sleepy Time Activity

Let's play a name game. See if you know these special names.
1. What's the name of our Creator?
2. What's your best friend's name?
As you go to sleep, name some people who love you. Good night!

THE TEN COMMANDMENTS

1
2
3
4
5
6
7
8
9
10

16

For Keeps!

God said, "What God promises, he keeps." Numbers 23:19

Sophie Springly was always making promises she didn't keep. She promised to give her brother, Sam, two cookies, but she ate them herself. She promised to give Mia Chang her old wagon. But Sophie kept it instead. Sophie never kept her promises to give things away because she wanted to keep everything she had!

Mrs. Bode's Sunday school class had a special project. The children wanted to collect a hundred books to give away. Everyone promised to bring books. "I'll bring my favorite book!" promised Sophie. But when she got home, Sophie looked at her favorite book and decided to keep it. I know I promised, she thought, but it won't matter.

Next Sunday, Mrs. Bode counted the books. "Ninety-seven, ninety-eight, ninety-nine. . . . We're one book short!" Mrs. Bode said. Sophie gulped. She knew she had broken her promise and it *did* matter! Sophie wanted to keep her book, but she wanted to keep her promise even more. What could she do?

How many children do you see?

"I'm sorry," Sophie said to her teacher. "I wanted to keep my promise, but I also wanted to keep my book."

Mrs. Bode smiled and said, "Sometimes promises are hard to keep, Sophie. But God also makes promises. God has promised to help you. And since God always keeps his promises, we can trust his promise to be true. So with God's help, you can make a promise and keep it, too!"

Sophie smiled. "I *can* do that! I can make my promises and keep them, too! And I promise to bring my book to you." And she did—the very next Sunday!

What promise did Sophie keep?
Who helped Sophie keep her promise?

A Bible Story to Remember

Genesis 7:6–8:12

When we make a promise, we need to keep it. That way, other people can trust us to do what we say. God always keeps his promises. He kept his promise to Noah, and he will keep his promises to us, too. We can trust God to do what he promises because he loves us.

A Prayer to Pray

Dear God,
Your promises
are true,
so I will always
count on you.
Amen.

A Sleepy Time Activity

God gave the world a sign of one of his promises—a rainbow in the sky! Can you name all the colors in a rainbow? As you go to sleep, think about a sky full of rainbows. Remember how beautiful and true God's promises are. Sleep tight!

19

Rescue Poochie

God said, "I will save you." Jeremiah 30:10

Sam Springly wanted a dog more than anything. All his friends had pets. And Sam was old enough for a dog, wasn't he? But Daddy said, "No dogs!" And Mommy said, "Dogs track in mud." Still, oh! how Sam longed for a dog of his own!

One morning, Sam saw a dog sitting under the shade tree. The puppy was skinny and small and had a funny spot over one eye. Mommy said, "Leave him alone. He'll go home." But after school the little pooch was still there!

"Please, Mommy," begged Sam and Sophie. "Can he come in? He's so skinny and hungry!"

"Just for a bite to eat," said Mommy. "But we won't keep him. We have no use for pooches here!" Sam and Sophie gave the little dog a nibble of ham and a drink of water. With all their hearts, they wanted to keep him.

"EEEEeeeek!" squealed Mommy. A tiny mouse skittered under the table. The little dog sprang into action. He yipped and yapped and yipped some more, till he chased that mousie out the door!

Find three animals.

21

"Oh, little pooch! You saved me from that awful mouse!" laughed Mommy. "Maybe we *could* use a brave watchdog around this house!"

"Yay!" shouted Sam. "Poochie saved you from the mouse and now we can save Poochie and give him a house!"

"And a home," smiled Mommy, as she patted brave little Poochie.

Count the cookies.
Who saved Poochie when he needed help?

A Bible Story to Remember

Exodus 2:1-10

The Bible tells us that when baby Moses needed help, God watched over him and kept him safe. God wants us to trust him, too, when we have trouble and don't know what to do. He is faithful and will always be there to help and heal and guide and care.

A Prayer to Pray

Dear God,
Thanks so much
for always being there
to help me and love me
and show that you care.
Amen.

A Sleepy Time Activity

Let's play a quiet game. Name some ways you can help your family, a friend, or a pet. Each time you name a way, point to your heart and say, "Thank you, God, for your help!" Think of how God saves you from trouble every day. Night-night.

The Helpers Club

God said, "You may serve me." Jeremiah 15:19

The kids were bored—there was nothing to do. "It's too hot to play," said Max Popple lazily. "Too hot," agreed Sophie Springly. Mia Chang petted Stormy while little Polly Popple tried to catch the kitten's swishing tail.

"Hi!" said Jimmy Lopez, riding up on Schnickelfritz. "What's going on?" he asked. "Just a lot of nothing," said Sam Springly. "Good!" said Jimmy, "You can help me clean up Mr. Morisky's sidewalk. There are leaves and papers all over after the storm last night. It will be fun!"

"Cleaning is fun?" asked Sophie. "Sure," said Jimmy. "It's fun to help others. Hey! We could even form a helpers club. Let's start right away!"

So the kids jumped up on that very hot day and discovered that helping can be as fun as play. They swept the sidewalk of the store, tossed out the papers, then did more! They polished the windows and dusted shelves; they did things for others instead of themselves.

What is Mia holding?

25

When they were finished, the store looked snappy. And though they were hot, all the kids felt happy!

Mr. Morisky smiled, "Thanks for your help! Now how about some ice cream for the Helpers Club?"

"Ice cream would be great!" said Jimmy, and all the kids nodded their heads in happy agreement. Then Jimmy said, "But the best part of serving is that when we serve others, we also get to serve God!"

Who's licking ice cream?
How did the Helpers Club serve God?

A Bible Story to Remember

Exodus 3:1-15

God chose Moses to be his special helper. But anyone can serve others. There are many ways to help people. We can sweep, paint, clean, or even say kind words and pray! Serving others is what God wants us to do. And when we serve others with love, we serve God, too!

A Prayer to Pray

Dear God,
Please help me
look for ways
to serve others
all my days.
Amen.

A Sleepy Time Activity

Night-Light wants to draw pictures! Draw a picture of how you can serve God and others in some special way. As you go to sleep, hold your picture and thank God for the joy that serving brings. Sleep tight!

Safe from the Storm

God said, "I will save you." Jeremiah 30:10

Crashhh! BOOM! What a rainstorm it was! But Max and Polly Popple were cozily playing in Max's room upstairs. Oh, they had made a marvelous mess! There were blocks and books all over the floor, an electric train, a flashlight, and more! Two-year-old Polly giggled as she and Max stacked up the blocks. Max was putting the last block on top when—CRASHHH-BOOOOM—everything went dark in Max's room!

"Waaaa!" wailed Polly. Max whispered, "Wow, it's dark!" Polly wailed even louder, "WaaAAA!"

Max knew Mommy and Daddy were downstairs, so he wasn't afraid. He didn't want Polly to be afraid either. Max wanted to help Polly. "Don't be afraid, Polly. It will be all right! See? Here's my flashlight. I'll flip on the light!" Max turned on his flashlight and Polly quit crying.

What's on the top shelf?

"Let's pretend we're crossing the Red Sea!"
said Max. They tiptoed around the building blocks
and scooted over the crayons and socks. Max and Polly
really had fun, and when Daddy appeared, all the lights
flickered on!

"I led Polly across the Red Sea and here to the
door as safe as can be!" shouted Max. Polly giggled and
clapped her hands. "Max helped!" shouted Polly.

Daddy smiled at their happy faces and at the sea of
toys scattered over the floor. "Now you and Polly can clean
up the sea and put it away as neat as can be!" he laughed.

Find the train.
Why do you think Max wanted to help Polly?

A Bible Story to Remember

Exodus 14

When Moses and the people came to the Red Sea, God helped them cross as safe as could be. God is with us and he'll help us, too. That's nice to know, isn't it? So if you're afraid, day or night, just call on God and you'll feel all right!

A Prayer to Pray

Dear God,
Thank you for
your saving care
and for promising me
you'll always be there.
Amen.

A Sleepy Time Activity

Night-Light wants to play a game to remind us how God keeps us safe. Tell how we can stay safe in these situations: at a swimming pool; crossing a street; in a crowded store. Think of how God keeps you safe all the time. Good night!

Cool Rules

God said, "Obey me." Jeremiah 7:23

Max Popple and Sophie Springly were in Miss Chalkdust's class. Sophie liked school and her pretty teacher, but Max wasn't sure. "Too many rules!" frowned Max. "Put your toys away when you're done. And always remember not to run. Yuck! Too many rules!"

Miss Chalkdust said, "Rules keep us healthy and happy all day. Rules are good things we can obey!" Still, Max wasn't sure he liked so many rules.

Sophie and Max were busy in school. They learned all about letter B and how to count 1-2-3. They explored the science nook, fed the fish, and read a book. Then the teacher said, "It's picture painting time!"

"Oh, boy!" shouted Max, running to get his paint shirt. But in his hurry, Max tripped over the toy truck he had forgotten to pick up. He knocked his knee and spilled red paint all over his new shirt.

"Ouch!" said Max. "My knee has an owie and now so does my shirt!"

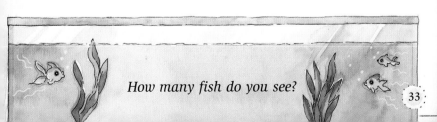

How many fish do you see?

33

Max thought about all those rules. Then Max put away the toy truck. Max cleaned up the spilled paint. Finally, Max smiled and said, "Miss Chalkdust, can we make one more rule?"

"What rule is that, Max?" asked Miss Chalkdust.

"The rule is: Whether you're at home or at school, ALWAYS obey EVERY rule!" Max said. Miss Chalkdust smiled and put the new rule on the bulletin board right then.

Count the pencils.
Why should Max have followed the rules?

A Bible Story to Remember

Deuteronomy 5

Night-Light has some rules to follow: Don't fly too high and always turn your light on in the dark. Night-Light knows about God's rules, too. God gave Moses ten special rules for us to obey. God gives us rules to keep us safe at work and play.

A Prayer to Pray

Dear God,
Please help me
to obey you
in everything
I say and do.
Amen.

A Sleepy Time Activity

Let's play a game. Think of some signs that tell us what to do (stop sign, green light, etc.). Tell what rules go with the signs and how the rules keep us safe. Then think of ways God's rules keep us safe. Sleep tight!

36

Dandy Candy

God said, "Love your neighbor." Leviticus 19:18

Jimmy Lopez lived in the blue house on the corner. He was seven years old and the big kid on the block. Jimmy liked to share his pony, Schnickelfritz, with his friends. He let them have bouncy rides on the pony's scruffy back.

One sunny day, Jimmy rode Schnickelfritz to Mr. Morisky's store to look at all the delicious candy. Mmmm, he wanted to taste it all! Jimmy rushed home and shook his piggy bank. Clinkety-clink. A pile of coins fell onto his floor. "I can buy LOTS of candy with this!" Jimmy said.

And so he did. He bought chocolate drops and peppermint twirls, lemony lollipops and sugary swirls. My, oh my, what a lot of candy! Then Jimmy saw his friends walking down the street. He said, "They'll want too much of my candy treat! Then what will be left for me to eat?" So he quickly started gobbling up his sweet snacks.

"Ummm-ooohhh!" groaned Jimmy after a bit. "I don't feel good. I think I feel sick! I was greedy eating all of this sticky goo. I should have shared like God wants me to!"

Count the pets and people.

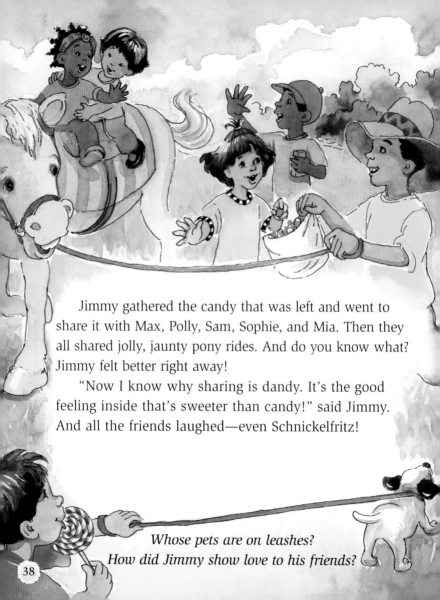

Jimmy gathered the candy that was left and went to share it with Max, Polly, Sam, Sophie, and Mia. Then they all shared jolly, jaunty pony rides. And do you know what? Jimmy felt better right away!

"Now I know why sharing is dandy. It's the good feeling inside that's sweeter than candy!" said Jimmy. And all the friends laughed—even Schnickelfritz!

Whose pets are on leashes?
How did Jimmy show love to his friends?

A Bible Story to Remember

Ruth 1

Ruth and Naomi were good friends. They helped and shared with one another and showed God's love to each other. God has given us lots of things, but not just to keep for ourselves! Oh, no! That's not neighborly! When we take the time to share, we show God's love!

A Prayer to Pray

*Dear God,
Please help me always
to give and share,
and spread your
warm love everywhere!
Amen.*

A Sleepy Time Activity

Let's play a quiet game. Put your hand over your heart and name a person and one thing you can share. Maybe a cookie with your sister? Feel your heart beat and remember that God always shares his love with us. Night-night!

Pretty Pony

God said, "The Lord looks at the heart." 1 Samuel 16:7

Today was the Pretty Pet Show and Jimmy Lopez was taking Schnickelfritz. "He's the prettiest pet there is!" said Jimmy proudly to Sam Springly. Sam said, "I don't know if he's pretty, but he sure is chubby!" Schnickelfritz nuzzled Sam and Poochie. "And he's as nice as nice can be!" laughed Sam.

Such a lot of pets were there that day. Look—there's a puppy and kitten at play. There's a lizard, a fish in a bowl, and even a hedgehog—he's adorable!

"Schnickelfritz just has to win the prize for the best pet!" Jimmy said. Finally, the contest judge came to see Schnickelfritz. The judge frowned and looked over the scruffy pony. "Well, he seems pretty chubby for a pony, I see—and his coat isn't as glossy as it could be. His tail is a bit of a tangle, you know? Still there's something about him—but I just don't know . . ." Jimmy held his breath and waited.

How many pets are there?

All at once, Schnickelfritz tickled the judge's ear with a friendly whiffle, then whinnied happily. The judge scratched his ear and laughed. "Well, he may not be the prettiest pet, but he's the friendliest pony I've ever met!" smiled the judge, and he handed Jimmy a blue ribbon.

Jimmy hugged his friendly pony. "Looks aren't everything," Jimmy said with pride. "It's not so important how we look, but what we're like on the inside!"

Who is tickling the judge's ear?
Why did Schnickelfritz win a ribbon?

A Bible Story to Remember

1 Samuel 16:1-13

When God sees us, he doesn't just look
at the outside. He looks at our hearts!
God looked at David's heart, and not
his size, when he chose him to be king.
God sees our hearts, too—what we feel,
think, and dream. And what's on the
inside is more beautiful than anything!

A Prayer to Pray

Dear God,
Please help me
always be
the kind of person
you like to see!
Amen.

A Sleepy Time Activity

Let's look at our hearts. Cut a heart out of paper and put it
near your bed. As you go to sleep, look at your heart cutout
and think of ways God can help you be beautiful on the
inside. Good night!

Sam's Bully

God said, "I will make you strong." Isaiah 45:5

Sam Springly was worried. "Rat" Raymond, the class bully, was picking on Sam's friends. This big boy called himself "Rat" because he liked to tease the scaredy "mice" in his class. Nobody liked Rat Raymond.

"Go ahead and run! Everyone's scared of me!" Rat called when kids ran from him.

It made Sam angry that Rat was mean to other kids. But no one could stop Rat from being such a meany, right?

That night, Sam prayed, "Dear God, there's a giant problem at school. That bully Rat Raymond is breaking every rule! Please help me be strong and know what to do, 'cuz even ol' Rat is not bigger than you!" What could Sam do? Would God help Sam be strong and wise, even though Rat was twice his size?

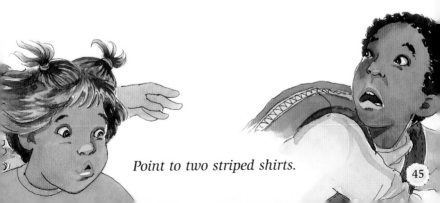

Point to two striped shirts.

45

The next day, Sam felt brave. At lunch he walked right up to Rat Raymond and held out a cupcake. "Here, Rat, it's for you! I'll be your friend if you'd like me to!"

Rat stared. "No one ever wanted to be my friend," he said. "Thanks! And by the way, my real name's Rick."

Suddenly the giant meany disappeared. Sam learned that Rick Raymond was a nice guy! And what else did Sam learn? No problem is too big for our God above—just look what can happen when we share his love!

What did Sam share?
Who helped Sam be strong, brave, and wise?

A Bible Story to Remember

I Samuel 17:1-50

When David brought down the giant Goliath with just a stone, he discovered that God is bigger than anything or anyone! When we're worried or afraid, all we have to do is ask for God's help. God loves us. He will answer by helping us be strong, wise, and brave!

A Prayer to Pray

Dear God,
Thank you for being
faithful and true.
No problem is ever
too big for you!
Amen.

A Sleepy Time Activity

Would you like to play a game with Night-Light? Take turns naming big and small things. As you go to sleep, thank God that no problem is too big or small for him! Night-night!

Thanks from the Heart

God said, "Show thanks to God." Psalm 50:14

Valentine's Day was near and the neighborhood kids were excited! "Let's do something different this year," said Max. Mia jumped up and said, "Maybe we could make the biggest valentine in the world and give it to someone who's never had a valentine!"

"But everyone has had a valentine!" said Sophie.

The kids thought for a moment, then Jimmy Lopez said, "You know, God invented love but I don't think *he's* ever had a valentine."

"That's sad," said Sophie. "I know! Let's give God the biggest valentine there ever was! We can tell God we love him and thank him for his love, too!"

The group got to work right away. The kids colored and cut and snipped hearts all day; they painted and pasted—it was more fun than play! They cut pretty pink ribbons and fancy white laces until the love in that card matched the love on their faces!

Count the hearts.

49

Then they wrote a thank-you note to God. Here's what it said:

"Dear God, it's almost Valentine's Day,
And there's something special we want to say.
No one says it quite enough
When they're saying all that mushy stuff—
But we want to give our thanks to you
For all you say and all you do!
Thank you for our families and sunshine above—
But most of all, thank you for inventing love!"
Love, Mia, Max, Jimmy, Sophie, and Sam

How did the friends thank God?
Who is shown on the thank-you note?

A Bible Story to Remember

Psalm 23

David worshiped and thanked God for
all the things he did for him. Think
of all the nice things God does for us!
He has given us loving friends and
families, his words in the Bible, and so
much more. Let's thank God and say,
"We love you!"

A Prayer to Pray

Dear God,
I give my thanks
to you today
and through
my whole life, too.
Amen.

A Sleepy Time Activity

Night-Light wants to play a quiet game. Cut out five paper
hearts. Take turns holding the hearts and naming things to
be thankful for. As you fall asleep, hold the hearts and tell
God how much you love him. Sleep tight!

An Answer in Time!

God said, "I will answer you." Jeremiah 33:3

Mia Chang felt awful. Grandma couldn't come to Mia's dance recital on Saturday. Grandma's car was broken and she lived two hours away.

"I'm sorry, Mia," said Grandma on the phone. "I really wanted to see my chick-a-baby dance! Maybe if we pray, God will find a way to get me there," she said. Mia loved Grandma and wanted to see her. And Mia especially wanted Grandma to see her pretty dance costume. But could God fix Grandma's car if they prayed?

"God answers prayers," Sophie Springly said to Mia. "I learned that in Sunday school! Why don't you pray?"

So Mia prayed, "Dear God, I love my Grandma so; I want to see her, don't you know? But Grandma lives away so far—could you please fix her car? Amen."

Mia prayed and prayed. Then Mia waited and waited for God to answer. Monday, Tuesday, Wednesday's near; Thursday, Friday, Saturday's here! Would God really answer? Did God really hear?

What animals do you see?

On Saturday afternoon, Mia was still waiting for God's answer. She put on her pretty pink-and-purple dance costume and was ready to leave the house when . . . Grandma arrived!

"My car is still broken and just won't go, so I took a bus to come see your show!" laughed Grandma. "Wow!" Mia shouted. "God did hear my prayer and he answered, too! Thank you, God—and Grandma, I love you!"

Count the pink flowers.
Tell how God answered Mia's prayers.

A Bible Story to Remember

Daniel 6

God promises to hear and answer our
prayers. God answered Daniel's prayers
and kept him safe in the lion's den. God
will answer us in his own way—but not
always the way we think he will. God's
answers are never late; his answers are
perfect and worth the wait!

A Prayer to Pray

Dear God,
I'm glad you
answer prayer
and that
you're always there.
Amen.

A Sleepy Time Activity

Night-Light wants to draw a picture and you can, too.
Draw a picture of something you pray for and want God
to answer. Then say a prayer and thank God for the
answer that he will send you. Night-night.

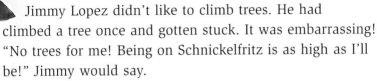

Up a Tree!

God said, "Be strong and brave." Joshua 1:7

Jimmy Lopez didn't like to climb trees. He had climbed a tree once and gotten stuck. It was embarrassing! "No trees for me! Being on Schnickelfritz is as high as I'll be!" Jimmy would say.

One Saturday, Mia and her kitten, Stormy, came to see Jimmy. The sun was out and birds sang in the apple trees. Jimmy let Mia and Stormy ride Schnickelfritz around the yard. My, what fun they had, until Stormy saw a bird! Quick as a wink, the fluffy black kitten scampered up the tree.

"Stormy!" called Mia. "You come down right away!" But Stormy didn't move. Stormy was stuck! "Meeowwww!" cried Stormy.

"Oh, my poor kitty—you look so blue! Jimmy, he's stuck! What will we do?" said Mia. Jimmy gulped. He was scared to climb trees—even short ones! Who could help Jimmy be strong and brave? Jimmy talked quietly to God. "Could you make me brave, God? Would you stay with me? I need to be brave to climb up this tree!"

Count the birds.

Then Jimmy took a deep breath and trusted God. Jimmy kneeled on Schnickelfritz and got a boost, then climbed and stretched until he reached Stormy in his leafy roost! Jimmy carried Stormy down the tree and safely into Mia's arms.

Mia hugged Stormy and said, "Thank you, Jimmy! You're as brave as can be!"

"That's 'cuz God was climbing with me!" smiled Jimmy.

What animals do you see?
How did trusting God help Jimmy?

A Bible Story to Remember

Esther 4:9–5:8; 7

Because God helped Queen Esther to be brave, she was able to keep his people safe. We can trust God to make us brave, too! God doesn't want us to be afraid. We just need to ask for God's help and then trust in his power and strength!

A Prayer to Pray

Dear God,
Thank you for making
me strong every day.
And help me to keep
trusting in you.
Amen.

A Sleepy Time Activity

Night-Light wants to play a quiet game. Take turns telling things you're worried about or afraid of, and then say, "God said, 'Be strong and brave.'" As you fall asleep, thank God for being strong and for helping you be brave, too! Sleep tight.

I'm With You!

God said, "I am with you." Jeremiah 30:11

Mia was sad. Her daddy was going away on a trip. It would be four whole days before she would see Daddy again. Monday, Tuesday, Wednesday, Thursday—could she stand having Daddy away?

"Why can't I go with you?" Mia asked as Daddy packed. Daddy smiled. "Because I need you to be my helper here at home and keep Mommy and Joe from being lonesome!" he said, hugging Mia.

"But who will keep me from being lonesome?" sniffed Mia. Then Daddy pulled an unusual coin from his special box. The coin had tiny bits of red, yellow, and green on one side. It was a beautiful coin!

"When I was a little boy, Grandma gave me this coin when I felt lonesome. Now I think I'll give it to you!" said Daddy. "If you keep this coin and hold on to it tight, you can feel like I'm with you when I'm not in sight!"

Mia felt a little better. But would it feel like Daddy was *really* there with her?

Point to Daddy's suitcase.

61

Monday, Mia squeezed the coin all day. Tuesday, she flipped the coin to play. Wednesday, Mia took the coin to school and all the kids thought it was cool! Thursday, Mia shined the coin with care and before she knew it, Daddy was there!

"I had fun with our special coin, Daddy, and you were right! Even though you were far away, it felt like you were here each day!" shouted Mia, and she squeezed her coin and her Daddy.

How did Daddy help Mia even though he was away?
Point to Mia's special coin.

A Bible Story to Remember

Luke 2:4-7

The Bible tells us that God sent his
Son, Jesus, to be born in a stable.
God gave us Jesus to be with us and
to remind us that he is here helping us.
When we love God and Jesus, we're
never alone!

A Prayer to Pray

Dear God,
Thank you for
your loving care
and for sending Jesus
to always be there!
Amen.

A Sleepy Time Activity

Let's play a quiet game. Pass a gift bow back and forth and
take turns naming gifts God brings us through Jesus such
as love, help, and faith. Then cuddle your bow as you think
of how God and Jesus are with you even when you sleep!
Night-night.

Tied Up in Knots

Jesus said, "Learn from me." Matthew 11:29

"I can't do this!" pouted Sophie Springly. "I need someone to teach me!" Sophie was learning to tie her shoes—or at least, she was *trying* to learn.

"Wear slip-ons," suggested Mia Chang, showing Sophie her new shoes. "Wear cowboy boots!" shouted Jimmy Lopez, trotting by on Schnickelfritz. But Sophie wanted to tie her shoes herself. Sophie sighed as Poochie gave her a friendly lick. "You're lucky you don't wear shoes, Poochie!" said Sophie, patting her furry friend.

"I'll teach you," said Sam, sitting beside his sister. Sophie wrinkled her nose. "You, a *teacher*?" she asked. "But you're just a kid!"

"Jesus taught others once when he was just a kid!" said Sam. "Just listen to me and follow the directions." Then Sam told Sophie a story of a funny bunny with two shoelace ears.

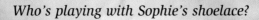

Who's playing with Sophie's shoelace?

65

First Sam tied a half knot, then he said,
"Here's the left ear . . .
Here's the right . . .
Cross the ears, tuck one under—
Then pull the bow tight!"

Then Sophie tried. "Hmmm . . . Cross the ears, tuck one under and pull it through . . . Look, Sam! I tied my shoe!" Sam cheered and Poochie wagged all over. "When you listen to teaching that's right on the dot, the questions you have won't tie you in knots!" laughed Sam.

Count all the ears you see.
What did Sam teach Sophie?

66

A Bible Story to Remember

Luke 2:41-52

Jesus is our best teacher! Even when Jesus was young, he taught others at the temple about God and his love. Jesus was sent from God above to teach us about forgiveness and love. Jesus wants us to learn from him, too, and obey every lesson in all we do!

A Prayer to Pray

Dear Jesus,
Thank you for your
lessons in love and
all that you teach me
of my Father above!
Amen.

A Sleepy Time Activity

You can play a quiet learning game with Night-Light. See if you can learn this Scripture verse. Jesus said, "Learn from me" (Matthew 11:29). As you go to sleep, thank Jesus for being our best teacher—and our best friend! Sleep tight.

In a Pickle!

Jesus said, "Do all things that are right." Matthew 3:15

Max Popple was excited. Today was Aunt Martha's surprise birthday party. Mommy wanted everything just right! Max helped set the table with the best dishes while Mommy poured the cake batter into the pans. Everything looked so nice. "Please put the pickles on the table, Max," said Mommy as she went to answer the phone. But when Max picked up the pickle dish, out popped a pickle into a pan of cake batter!

"Uh-oh," said Max, quickly trying to think what to do. But before he could decide, Mommy came back and whisked the cake pans into the oven. "There!" smiled Mommy. "Now everything is just right!"

But not *everything* was right! Max thought about that little pickle and worried. "If I tell Mommy now she might be mad and Aunt Martha's surprise will be awfully bad. Maybe the pickle will melt and just go. I won't say a word and then no one will know!" But Max knew. And God knew, too. Would Max do the right thing, like God would want him to?

Count the pickles.

After dinner, Aunt Martha blew out the birthday candles. Mommy cut the cake. And Max held his breath. That little pickle is there in the cake, he thought. Nobody knows I made a mistake! But someone did know. Max knew. He felt awful. He knew he had not done the right thing. What should he do? Was it too late?

Then Max told the truth. He said he was sorry. Did Mommy get mad? No, not at all—absolutely not! Instead she forgave Max right on the spot. And no, Aunt Martha's surprise was not *just* right. But Aunt Martha laughed, "Pickle-cake! I think I'll try a bite!"

Count the candles.
What did Max do that was wrong?

A Bible Story to Remember

Matthew 3:13-17

Max did the right thing when he told the truth. The Bible tells us that Jesus did the right thing when he was baptized. It's good for us to do what's right, too. When we do good things in love, we know God smiles from above!

A Prayer to Pray

Dear God,
Please help me always
to be just like you
and choose the right
thing in all that I do.
Amen.

A Sleepy Time Activity

Night-Light wants to play a game. Take turns making up choices and deciding what's the right thing to do. Tell a lie or tell the truth? Pick up your toys or leave a mess? As you fall asleep, think about the right things that Jesus did. Good night!

Follow the Leader

Jesus said, "Follow me." Matthew 4:19

It was a lovely summer day, just right for any kind of play! "Let's play Follow the Leader!" cried Jimmy Lopez. Mia Chang, Sophie Springly, and Max and Polly Popple shouted, "Good idea!" and hopped in line behind Jimmy.

"We'll take turns being the leader," explained Jimmy. "Follow me!" Jimmy led and everyone followed. They jumped after Jimmy to a red sandbox, walked around the rim, and across big rocks.

Then Mia led and everyone followed. They skipped with Mia past a rake and hoe. They hopped over a creek bed where water once flowed.

Then Max led and everyone followed. They climbed with Max up a short, steep hill and when he tiptoed down, they followed him still!

"Now me!" squealed Polly. Polly led and everyone followed. They paraded after Polly through a sprinkler-flood—right up to a puddle of . . .

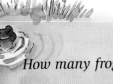

How many frogs can you find?

73

"Not *mud*!" laughed the kids. "Polly," said Sophie, "a good leader leads toward good things. C'mon, I'll show you how!" Sophie led and everyone followed. They marched after Sophie as best as they were able—right into her house and straight to the table.

"Pizza!" shouted the kids. Sophie's daddy had just set a freshly baked pizza out to cool. "Leading toward good things is what a good leader knows—and though I was the leader, I just followed my nose!" Sophie said.

Count the cups.
Tell what a good leader does.

A Bible Story to Remember

Matthew 4:18-20

Jesus leads us toward all good things such as love, forgiveness, eternal life, and faith. Jesus called special disciples to follow him. Now Jesus wants us to follow him, too. What a loving leader to follow!

A Prayer to Pray

Dear God,
Please help me follow
only you
and stick to your way
my whole life through.
Amen.

A Sleepy Time Activity

Night-Light wants to play a quiet game of Follow the Leader! Follow these directions: touch your nose; pat your toes; count to five; clap your hands three times; say "I'll follow Jesus!" Think of how nice it is to follow Jesus! Night-night.

Sophie the Samaritan

Jesus said, "Show mercy." Luke 6:36

It sure is hard to like everyone. Sophie Springly didn't like the new girl in her class—no, siree! The little girl broke Sophie's crayons and knocked over Sophie's building block tower. Then she scribbled on Sophie's beautiful painting! Sophie thought, I'm really mad. This is it! I don't think I like her one little bit!

Sophie had a shiny new bicycle and wanted to take it to school for show-and-tell. "Sam can walk with you," smiled Mommy. "Take care of your new bicycle!"

Sophie rode proudly, but when she reached school, the new girl ran up and said, "Your bike's really cool! Can I ride it? I can ride real good!" Before Sophie could answer, the girl rode off in a flash. But a moment later—oh, what a crash! The little girl ran into a tree, bumped the bike, and nicked her knee.

Sophie felt funny. She felt mad and a little glad. But there was another feeling Sophie had. Sophie felt sort of bad! She knew she should help the girl. But could she help someone she didn't really like?

How many squirrels are there?

Sophie thought about the story she'd heard in Sunday school. It was the Bible story about the man who was left hurt on the road and the good Samaritan who helped him. Sophie thought and then she decided. She *could* help that little girl! Sophie ran to help her. The surprised little girl said, "You really want to help me?"

"Sure," smiled Sophie, feeling friendlier. "You need help and I'm right here, too. I will give my help to you. I'm glad you think my bike is cool, and you can try it again after school!"

Count the flowers.
Why did Sophie help the little girl?

A Bible Story to Remember

Luke 10:30-37

Jesus teaches us to love and care for all
people. To help us understand, Jesus
told about a Samaritan man who was
merciful to a stranger in need. Just like
the Samaritan man, we need to be kind
all the time—even to people who don't
treat us very well.

A Prayer to Pray

Dear God,
Please help me
always be
kind to those
who are mean to me.
Amen.

A Sleepy Time Activity

Night-Light wants to play a quiet game. Say a way to be
merciful and kind when someone breaks your favorite toy,
or calls you a name, or pushes you. As you go to sleep,
think of how Jesus loves us all the time—no matter what!
Sleep tight.

Everyone's Invited

Jesus said, "Come to me." Matthew 19:14

Sophie and Mia were planning a tea party. They planned to set the table with their best plastic tea sets. They planned to serve graham crackers with icing and candy sprinkles. And they planned to pour apple juice from their fancy teapot.

"Mommy says we can't have tea, so juice sounds just as good to me!" smiled Sophie. "But who can we invite?"

The girls thought for a moment. Then Mia said, "We won't invite babies 'cuz they cry a lot. And they might tip over the tea party pot!"

"And we won't invite grown-ups to sip tea or eat, 'cuz they might not like our sprinkly treats!" added Sophie.

"What about boys?" asked Mia.

"Boys?" said Sophie. "We won't invite boys to our afternoon tea—they don't know how to sip tea politely!"

"Who can we invite?" wondered Mia. "There's nobody left!"

Count the plates and cups.

The girls thought and thought. Then Sophie said, "Who would Jesus invite to a party or tea? Surely he would invite everyone he'd see!"

Mia smiled and nodded. "If Jesus would invite everyone, including you and me, then we'll invite everyone to our neighborhood tea!" she said.

"Well, if we're going to invite everyone in the neighborhood," laughed Sophie, we'd better get a bigger teapot!"

How many bracelets do you see?
Who did the girls invite to come to their party?

A Bible Story to Remember

Matthew 19:13-15

Jesus showed his love when he told the children to come to him. Jesus loves us and wants us all to know and follow him. He invites us all to come and learn about our Father above—young or old or shy or bold—Jesus wants everyone to share his love!

A Prayer to Pray

Dear God,
I'm so glad
you want me near
and like to be
with me right here!
Amen.

A Sleepy Time Activity

Night-Light wants to play a quiet game. Pretend you're going to have a party with Jesus and name all the people you would invite! As you go to sleep, think about how much Jesus wants you to share his love! Good night.

The Giving Flower

Jesus said, "Give to God." Matthew 22:21

Jimmy Lopez felt like he'd won a million dollars! He woke up to a sunshiny day full of playful breezes. Jimmy went outside and stooped to pick the prettiest flower in the garden. It was easy to love the whole world on such a lovely morning!

But not everyone was happy. Jimmy's neighbor, Mrs. Flutterby, was feeling flustered. She had burned her best cinnamon rolls. Jimmy saw her frown and went over to give Mrs. Flutterby the beautiful flower. "Here's something I can give to you—it'll help you smile the whole day through!" Jimmy said. Mrs. Flutterby laughed. "Thanks for giving me a smile!" she said happily.

From that moment on, each minute and hour, the beautiful blossom was a busy flower! It traveled here and was given there. It brought love and smiles everywhere!

Mrs. Flutterby gave the flower to her friend Mrs. Click, to give her a smile since her daughter was sick. And when sick little Sarah was feeling quite sad, her mommy gave her the flower to make her feel glad!

Can you find six butterflies?

85

The giving went round in a circle all day, and came back to the start when Jimmy went to play.

"I'm sorry you're sick, Sarah. I feel bad," Jimmy said. Then Sarah gave Jimmy the flower. "This will help you feel glad!" she said.

Jimmy looked at the flower, then laughed with joy. "Giving love away is easy, I've found. And when we give love to others, it comes back around!"

How did Jimmy give to others?
Who gave the flower back to Jimmy?

A Bible Story to Remember

Luke 21:1-4

The Bible tells of a poor woman who cheerfully gave God all she had—two copper coins. We can give cheerfully to God, too. When we give others our help and caring, we are also giving to God. Giving love is easy to do, and that love will come back to you!

A Prayer to Pray

Dear God,
Please help me have
a loving heart.
That is where the
giving starts!
Amen.

A Sleepy Time Activity

Let's make giving flowers! Cut out a paper flower and use crayons to decorate it. As you go to sleep, look at the flower and think about all the love you can give to God. Then give your pretty flower to someone in the morning! Sleep tight.

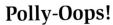

Polly-Oops!

Jesus said, "Forgive them." Luke 23:34

Little Polly Popple was always dropping, bopping, bumping, breaking, and tripping over everything! "Oops," Polly said when she spilled her milk. "Oops," Polly said when she broke Mommy's vase. "Oops-oops!" Polly said when she flushed Daddy's tie down the potty. Mommy smiled patiently. "She's too little to know what's best to do," she said. Daddy laughed. "She's our little Polly-oops," he said, hugging his little girl.

Polly's brother, Max, had a remote-controlled truck. Max would hold the remote control and make the truck turn right and left, then spin around. It would go up hills and rumble down. Max loved his truck and Polly loved to watch Max drive.

One day Max was wheeling his truck across the driveway. Polly held her juice and laughed as the truck spun around her feet in funny loops. "Zoom, zoom, go!" clapped Polly. But when she clapped, down went the cup—and a very juicy truck came to a stop!

"Oops," whispered Polly. "Poll-YYYY!" Max groaned.

What bugs do you see?

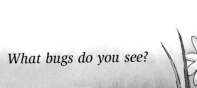

"Look what you've done!" Max said. "You've
ruined my truck and all of our fun!" Max was mad—
but he also knew in his heart that Polly didn't mean
to drop her juice. Max thought about how Jesus forgave
others. Then Max looked deeper into his heart and knew
he loved Polly, even if she caused trouble sometimes.

Polly's bottom lip was sticking out and her eyes were
so, so sad. "Polly-oops," he said, as a tear slid down her
cheek. Max gathered up all the love in his heart and said,
"I forgive you, Polly-oops! Now let's fix our truck and do
some loopy-loops!"

Count four flowers.
Why did Max forgive Polly?

A Bible Story to Remember

Matthew 27:11-66

Jesus died to forgive our sins and to show us God's love never ends. Jesus wants us to love and forgive, too. When we forgive with love, we grow closer to God in heaven above!

A Prayer to Pray

Dear God,
Please help me be
just like you
and show forgiveness
to others, too.
Amen.

A Sleepy Time Activity

Take turns remembering times you needed forgiveness or you forgave someone. How did you feel? How did love help you forgive someone? As you fall asleep, think of how Jesus loves and forgives us when we ask him. Night-night!

Love Is Alive

Jesus said, "I will be with you always." Matthew 28:20

Jimmy Lopez was very sad. It was Easter morning and he missed his daddy. Jimmy's daddy died when Jimmy was five. Jimmy missed him a lot. "Mommy," asked Jimmy, "why did Daddy have to die? I feel so sad inside." Mommy hugged Jimmy and said, "Jesus' friends asked the same question and felt the same way when Jesus died on the cross. They had to trust God's plans. And they had to remember all the love Jesus gave them."

"I can remember Daddy's love," said Jimmy. Mommy said, "Why don't we look at our special pictures and remember!" She got the picture book out. Jimmy pointed and said, "Here's when Daddy and I washed the car—and the time that we rode on a bus oh-so-far!"

"And remember the time we all went to the zoo?" Mommy asked. Jimmy laughed and said, "When Daddy hopped me around like a big kangaroo! And here's the day that we cooked lunch outside and Daddy gave me my first Schnickelfritz ride!"

Point to all the pictures.

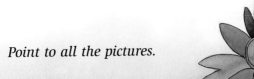

93

Then Jimmy stopped and smiled. "This is like the first Easter," he said. "Jesus' friends found out that Jesus was alive and would always be with them. And now I know that even though Daddy's not alive, his memory can live with me and his love stays alive in my heart!"

Jimmy's mom smiled and said, "Let's take some time before we go to church and thank God for his love, and for giving us special memories." Then Jimmy and Mommy prayed together.

Whose hat does Jimmy have?
Why was Jimmy sad?

A Bible Story to Remember

Luke 24:1-12

Jesus died to forgive our sins. That was very sad. But we can be happy knowing that Jesus is alive today. He helps us in every way, even when people we love die. He helps us to trust God's plans and to remember his love.

A Prayer to Pray

Dear God,
I'm happy more
than I can say
because I know
you're alive today!
Amen.

A Sleepy Time Activity

Let's play a remembering game. Take turns remembering the following times: a happy time; a time you were sick; your favorite toy; a trip you took. As you fall asleep, remember how good it is to know that Jesus is alive and loving you! Good night.

Spread the Good News

Jesus said, "Tell the Good News." Mark 16:15

Sophie Springly was excited! She had good news to tell. Who could she tell her news to? Hey, there was Ginny James playing ball! Surely she'd like to hear this good news. Sophie skipped, stopped, then sat. Sophie had great news today, but what exactly would she say?

Just then, Sam Springly and Max Popple appeared. They were bouncing basketballs. "What's up, Sophie?" asked Sophie's big brother. "You look worried."

Sophie sighed and said, "I wanted to tell Ginny James my important news, but I don't know how." "What news?" Sam asked. Sophie smiled. "It's the Good News about Jesus!" she said. Then her smile faded away. "But I don't know exactly what words I should say."

"That's easy!" said Max. "Tell Ginny that Jesus is our best friend—that he stays right beside us from beginning to end!" Sam smiled and joined in, "And you can tell her about Jesus' great love, and how he was sent here from God up above!" Then Sophie shouted happily, "And Jesus forgives us and cares in every way—that's what I'll tell her! That's what I'll say!"

Count the basketballs.

But when Sophie jumped up and turned around, Ginny James was nowhere to be found. "Well," sighed Sophie, "guess I'll just have to tell her some other time."

What a surprise Sophie had the next day at Sunday school! Who was sitting at the front table? Ginny James!

Ginny grinned at Sophie and said, "I know you thought I was gone yesterday, but I listened to what you all had to say. And Jesus sounded so awesome, I wanted to come to church today!"

Find three stars.
What good news did Sophie want to share with Ginny?

A Bible Story to Remember

Mark 16:15-20

When you have good news, you want to share it, don't you? It's important for everyone to know, love, and follow Jesus. That's why Jesus told his friends to go and tell others about him. Jesus wants everyone to know he's here to forgive and love us so!

A Prayer to Pray

Dear God,
Help me to be brave
and always tell the
Good News about you
that I love so well!
Amen.

A Sleepy Time Activity

Night-Light wants to play an echo game and you can play, too! Take turns saying something about Jesus and having the other person repeat it! As you go to sleep, think about all the wonderful things you can tell about Jesus. Night-night!

A Different Answer

Jesus said, "Ask and you will receive." John 16:24

Sam Springly was on his way to buy Daddy's birthday present. Sam was going to buy Daddy his favorite candy bar. "An ooey-gooey Choco-Crunch is the perfect gift!" Sam said as he walked up to Mr. Morisky's store. But when Sam reached in his pocket for the money, what did he find? A hole! Sam's money had fallen out!

Sam searched the sidewalk and checked under rocks; he looked in the grass and even his socks—but the money was gone. "What're you doing?" asked Jimmy Lopez, riding up on Schnickelfritz. Sam sadly said, "I lost the money for Daddy's candy bar. I don't know what to do."

Jimmy thought for a moment. "My Sunday school teacher says: When you don't know what to do, pray to God and he'll answer you!"

So Sam prayed, "Dear God, I lost my money and can't buy Daddy his gift. Could you send an answer? It would give me such a lift! Amen."

How many rocks do you see?

Suddenly, Sam spotted something shiny in the grass. "Maybe it's my money!" he shouted. But when Sam looked closer, it was only a candy bar wrapper. "Awww," said Sam, tossing the wrapper aside.

"Wait!" said Jimmy, "What did that wrapper say?" Sam looked again. "Good for one free Choco-Crunch bar!" shouted Sam. "Thank you, God, for hearing me and saving Dad's birthday! You gave me what I asked for—you just answered in a different way!" laughed Sam.

What did Sam ask for?
How did God answer Sam?

A Bible Story to Remember

Acts 12:5-19

When Peter was in jail, his friends asked God for help. God heard their prayers and helped Peter escape. When we ask for God's help, he will give us what we need! God may answer in a different way than we think he will, but we can trust that he will answer!

A Prayer to Pray

Dear God,
I'm so glad
you're always there
to hear and answer
every prayer.
Amen.

A Sleepy Time Activity

Night-Light wants to draw a picture and you can, too. Draw a picture of something you can ask God for. Then hold your picture as you go to sleep and know that God will answer you in his time and in his way! Good night.

A New Everything

Jesus said, "I am making everything new!" Revelation 21:5

Sam and Sophie Springly watched Daddy paint the spare room with blue paint. Mommy was hanging new curtains in the windows. "Why is Grandpa Springly coming to live with us?" asked Sophie. Mommy explained, "Because he needs a new home, Sophie, and he wants to be near people who love him."

"And because we want to share our family with Grandpa," smiled Daddy. "We can make room for Grandpa in our house and in our hearts! It will be a new family for Grandpa, in a new house with a new room."

"There's a new everything!" said Sam. A new carpet was on the floor and Daddy had hung a new wooden door. There were new pictures on the table by the bed, and a new chair cushion in cherry red.

"I wish I had a new place being fixed up for me!" said Sophie, looking around the room.

What colors do you see?

105

"You do!" said Daddy. "Jesus is preparing a new home for all of us in heaven. And someday we can all live with God in his mansion!"

"That's cool!" said Sam excitedly. Sophie sighed, "But I'd still like a new room now." "Well, we can do that!" Mommy laughed. "Run and put on your paint shirts. We'll paint your rooms, too."

"Yay!" shouted Sophie and Sam, getting their paint shirts. Sophie smiled and said, "A new room for Grandpa, a new room for us, and a whole new home in heaven! A new everything!"

How did the Springlys prepare Grandpa's new room? Point to the paintbrushes.

A Bible Story to Remember

Revelation 21:1–22:5

Grandpa has a new room, and we can have a new home in heaven! Jesus is in heaven preparing a place for us to live with God. We'll live in a beautiful new home filled with love, a new home in heaven with our Father above.

A Prayer to Pray

Dear God,
Thank you for making
everything new
and for promising that
I can live with you!
Amen.

A Sleepy Time Activity

Would you like to play a game with Night-Light? Take turns telling about your room in heaven and what you'd like to have new in it. Then as you go to sleep, thank Jesus for making a special home filled with love just for us. Night-night!

God bless you and good night!

Scripture Index